LES PARSONS

RESPONSE JOURNALS

HEINEMANN
Portsmouth, NH

© 1990 Pembroke Publishers Limited
528 Hood Road
Markham, Ontario
L3R 3K9

Published in the U.S.A. by
Heinemann Educational Books, Inc.
361 Hanover Street
Portsmouth, NH 03801-3959
ISBN (U.S.) 0-435-08517-4

Library of Congress Catalog Card Number 90-117341

Canadian Cataloguing in Publication Data

Parsons, Les, 1943-
  Response journals

Includes bibliographical references,
ISBN 0-921217-41-2

1. Reading (Elementary) - Language experience
approach. 2. Language arts (Elementary). I. Title.

LB1573.33.P37 1989   372.4'14   C89-095172-1

Editor: Art Hughes
Design: John Zehethofer
Cover Photography: Ajay Photographics

Printed and bound in Canada
9 8 7 6 5 4

Contents

Foreword

Response Journals was written for the classroom teacher. Although grounded in current response theory, the basic, pragmatic approach recognizes the realities facing classroom teachers, especially the most fundamental of realities - evaluation. To be truly effective, response journals depend on a comprehensive system of formative and summative evaluation. Right from the start, students need to be part of the total process of using response journals. They need to know what they are, why and how they will be used, and most importantly, how they will be evaluated. For that reason, a number of specific and practical formative and summative evaluation instruments have been included for teachers to use.

Response Journals begins by clearing up the confusion between a relatively limited classroom strategy known commonly as journal writing and the multidimensional, learning/teaching tool called response journals. Teachers are then taken step-by-step through a comprehensive system that includes ready-to-use pages of directions for students and sample student responses. From suggestions for reading and literature programs to techniques for approaching media studies and co-operative learning strategies, *Response Journals* offers practitioners a down-to-earth handbook for implementing a whole language program based on personal response.

1 * Responding to journals

"I've tried journals and they don't work!"
"We did journals last year."
"I'm tired of journals!"

Many people are tired of hearing about journals, and they have a right to be. Unfortunately, they're tired of journals for the wrong reasons! Teachers often report that their students dislike writing regularly in a journal, that their entries tend to be repetitive in topic, treatment, and detail, and that they write as little as possible. Many of these problems stem from a confusion over what journals really are, how they should be used and evaluated, and the place of journal writing in the total language program.

A few years ago, as the "writing as process" approach took hold, the concept of "free writing" became popular. Students everywhere were required to keep "journals" of daily, spontaneous, private writing. Some teachers were reluctant even to read the entries without the student's permission. The problem, of course, was what to do with the volume of what was essentially private matter.

Enforced diary-keeping

After the novelty wore off, the enthusiasm for this kind of writing quickly dried up, but the practice continued. Entries tended to degenerate into simple narratives detailing what the students did the night before, what they had for breakfast, or what rock groups they liked

1

best. Eventually, the practice became a kind of enforced diary-keeping, disliked by everyone involved. Some teachers were able to adapt writing in journals to fill specific needs in their programs; most teachers, however, were left wondering why so much precious classroom time had to be devoted to such a limited strategy.

The kind of response journal described in this book is different. Although the essentials of personal response theory have become well-known and are changing the way we ask students to respond to their reading, the role of response journals in this process is often neglected, mainly because people still equate the term "journal" with its former, limited, and problematic use.

By combining the most useful aspects of learning logs and work diaries with contemporary response theory, response journals fill the need for a flexible and multi-dimensional learning-teaching tool to match the complex demands of current language arts and English programs. Formative and summative evaluation are integral components of this approach. Evaluation actually directs and supports the learning.

If your students are writing in journals for the sake of writing in journals, a fresh approach is in order. If your students are saying...

"I don't know what to write about!"

"How come we have to do journals again? We did them last year!"

"Can I do my own writing instead?"

"Does this count on my report card?"

... a fresh approach is *definitely* in order.

A response journal is not...

• a personal diary containing lists of favorite rock songs, breakfast menus, and "what I did last night!"

• a book in which students write responses that are never read, never discussed, and never evaluated

• a compendium of reactions to silent reading that has little connection with the rest of the language arts or English program

• another add-on to an already burgeoning curriculum!

A response journal is a notebook or folder in which students record their personal reactions to, questions about, and reflections on:

- what they read, view, listen to, and discuss;
- how they actually go about reading, viewing, listening, and discussing.

Just as a writing folder supports the writing process and is an essential tool in the formative and summative evaluation of both process and product, a response journal serves the reading process.

In an integrated program, however, the reading process combines elements of thinking, listening, speaking, writing, and viewing, as well as reading. The written response component of all of these elements can be combined and co-ordinated in the response journal.

Students reflect on what they've been reading, doing, and talking about and then reflect on how and why they respond as they do. As they work through the response program, they are able to develop the awareness of and, eventually, the commitment to their own learning processes necessary to help them develop effective reading strategies.

A response journal is ...

- a convenient, familiar, and flexible method for students to explore and reflect on their personal responses to such experiences as

  - independent reading
  - viewing a film or television program
  - listening to a readaloud
  - a small-group discussion

- a source book of ideas, thoughts, opinions, and first drafts which can be "mined" for later use in other contexts such as the writing folder

- a place to record observations and questions prior to a reading conference, and comments and suggestions derived from the conference

- a simple "tracking" device for students to record what and how much they've read, and, after a small-group discussion, their

---

individual perspectives on what was discussed or their roles in the discussion dynamics of the group

- a reference file to help both student and teacher monitor individual development and progress for both formative and summative evaluation purposes

- another way for individual students to "dialogue" in written form with their teacher or peers

Questions teachers ask about journals

Q. I'm already using journals and my students don't like them. Why should I use them even more?

A. "Personal" writing in the sense of "free writing" or "diary writing" is not the same as personal response. People often confuse the two terms.

"Free writing" is a technique with a specific and limited purpose. It is generally used for brief periods to increase the spontaneous flow of written material. Many teachers have all students keep "journals" of "free writing".

Response journals, on the other hand, could form the core of your language arts or English program. As you move through the chapters in this book, notice how many listening, speaking, reading, writing, and viewing functions are well served by the personal response process.

Q. Where do I find the time to use response journals?

A. Using response journals will save you time. As an all-purpose learning/teaching tool, a response journal will allow you to consolidate in one place a variety of your language arts or English components. This one, comprehensive file will make it easier for you to track, observe, and evaluate student language progress.

Q. How can you mark journals if you aren't even supposed to correct them?

A. Again, you're confusing the use of "free" or "personal" writing with the use of response journals. While it's true that response journals are not marked for mechanical accuracy or stylistic features, if used properly, they can form the basis on which you evaluate a student's language progress, summatively as well as formatively.

Q. How can students improve their writing if you don't point out their errors?

A. The revising/editing cycle of your writing-as-process program will help your students with the form of their writing. The response journal will allow students to shape, explore, clarify, and develop their thinking in their own language. In your total program, criteria are established and skills are taught.

Q. When can I find the time to write to every student?

A. You shouldn't be writing to every student! You can usually cover what you want to discuss with students about their journals in your regular, individual reading/writing conferences. If you need to offer written comments or suggestions to selected students, use the pads of small, "stick-on" message paper.

What about "Whole Language"?

Regardless of what educators mean by the phrase "writing as process", most teachers agree that writing is an active, creative process. What has been recognized only recently, however, is that reading is also an active, creative process. Those who advocate "writing as process" should also advocate "reading as process".

In fact, the so-called "whole language" movement rests on the simple assertion that "language as process" may incorporate at any one time aspects of listening, speaking, reading, writing, and viewing to achieve its purpose.

A commitment to "whole language" affirms, as well, that the act of processing language involves more than the communicating or recording of experience. Through language, we construct our sense of reality by clarifying, discovering, assessing, reflecting on, resolving, and refining what we really think and feel about experience.

This kind of learning/teaching philosophy emphasizes the weaving and integration of the various language "threads" within the single context of meaningful communication. A single writing task, for example, may engage a student in a range of discussion, composing, editing/revising, and reading tasks in a recursive and blended manner! With response journals, "the medium is the message." Response journals reflect the integrated nature of language use and the importance of a process orientation in a classroom setting.

The keeping of response journals supports but should never supplant the classroom language program. Through an appropriate balance of process and product in an integrated language program, teachers help students gain the confidence in and facility with language necessary to become independent, resourceful, and self-sufficient in the pursuit of their personal goals.

Using response journals to integrate language programs

Since response journals can serve many different functions, an overview of their uses may appear complicated. Even tracing how they integrate the reading, writing, listening, speaking, and viewing aspects of an English or language arts program can seem confusing. In practice, on the other hand, response journals simplify, streamline, and organize a comprehensive approach to personal response. The following functions are described in detail later on. For now notice the varied and flexible ways response journals can support your language arts or English program.

Response journals provide a means...

↓

• to evaluate individual progress

   - as a reference file to identify and describe process and assist with formative and summative evaluation

---

↓

• to explore personal responses

   - to independent and group reading experiences
   - to viewing experiences
   - after listening to readalouds
   - after a small-group discussion

↓

- to develop small-group discussions

  - reflecting on one's role in the discussion
    dynamic

↓

- to guide the student/teacher conference

  - with observations and questions prior to the
    conference
  - with suggestions derived from the conference

↓

- to track independent reading

  - recording what and how much is read

↓

- to maintain personal dialogues

  - writing back and forth to the teacher and/or
    peers

↓

- to develop a source book

  - of ideas for use in the writing folder

From such a diversity of functions, you can expect a wide variety of student responses. Throughout the book, you will find a number of sample responses to give you a concrete idea of what a response journal looks like when these learning objectives are translated into student outcomes. Spelling errors in the student responses have been corrected, but other stylistic features of student writing remain as they appeared in the original copy.

2 * Responding to reading and literature

In school, we "do" novels; we also "do" short stories, plays, and poetry. While many teachers seem unsure about how best to approach poetry, they usually seem confident about the accepted way to approach short stories and novels.

Do you "Do" literature?

From about Grade 4 on, teachers introduce students to such terms as theme, plot, setting, climax, and character study. In a typical novel study, for example, the entire class reads the same novel in small "chunks" and analyzes each chunk using these terms. Later, students usually have a chance to self-select a novel and examine it independently in the same manner.

The students' understanding of a novel is largely measured by examining their answers to teacher-made questions based on traditional "literary" categories. Students are marked on how well they understand the terms, whether they can apply that understanding to the novel under study, and how complete and detailed their answers are.

Most students are as familiar with this process as their teachers. They are also familiar with the pattern of beginning with short stories and poetry (usually from an anthology), moving on to a single novel chosen by the teacher, and closing the study with some small-group or individually-chosen novels. In this way, students learn to apply the terms to short fiction and then apply them together, as a class, to a longer literary selection. Finally, they have the opportunity to continue the approach with a self-selected novel.

But...

- Have you ever questioned whether this approach has any relevance to an actual understanding of literature?

- Have you ever wondered whether or not authors create books according to this blueprint?

- Do you ever wonder why it's necessary to teach these terms and follow this approach every year?

- Do you think there's any connection between some students' dislike of or inability to succeed in "English" and their dislike of or inability to cope with this kind of task?

- Do you ever wonder whether you could read, enjoy, and discuss books without resorting to this artificial approach? Do you wonder whether your students could?

If you don't "Do" literature, what do you do?

The problem with the traditional way of approaching literature in school is that "how" we go about it often gets in the way of "why" we're doing it. Take, for example, such "literary" terms as setting, plot, and character. Nonwriters may believe that writers start with these categories and then assemble their books like jigsaw puzzles. In that case, in order to fully understand an author's work, you would "undo" it. But writers don't write that way; certainly, literature isn't produced that way. Those terms may be useful and valid labels, but they are really only labels.

As well, how we approach literature in school should take into account what we know about reading. Overwhelming evidence indicates that reading programs should include the following components:

- material to match individual student interests and abilities

- frequent opportunities for students to self-select material

- a regular and significant amount of in-class time for students to simply read (as opposed to answering questions based on their reading)

- frequent opportunities to respond to material in a personally significant manner

- frequent opportunities for students to discuss with someone else what they're reading

- the flexibility to employ a variety of strategies to comprehend material.

These components are more easily accommodated if we allow the "why" of studying literature to set the direction for the "how".

Personal response unlocks literature

In simple terms, literature is the interactive and reciprocal process of making and sharing meaning. By comparing the parallel "reality" of a book with our own experience, we're able to expand and deepen the understanding we have of our own lives.

Looked at this way, the study of literature is actually a "life-skill". The key to the learning process comes when we try to make sense of an author's vision and consider any implications in that vision for ourselves. A book's value rests on its effect on the individual. Unfortunately, since we come to a book with our own distinctly individual and uniquely personal perspectives, including variables of language, background, and interests, no one book can attract or serve everyone at the same time.

When we do begin with a common experience, whatever we value or are intrigued by or are confused by in that experience will vary depending on the individual. Take the example of what happens when you see and discuss a film with a friend. When you finally get around to "picking away" at your feelings about the film, where you start seems totally reasonable and relevant to you but may appear obscure to your friend. The discussion proceeds in fits and starts, jumping here, there, and everywhere, as you both follow, share, and extend your own personal paths of perception, importance, and logic. A color motif might strike you while a recurring shape or image might catch your friend's attention. Your friend might focus on a similar, "real-life" experience he/she knows about while you've become distracted by a personal phobia encountered in the film. Eventually, you arrive at a heightened appreciation of the film and an understanding of the other person's point of view, often in spite of still disagreeing about the film.

The study of literature in schools needs to follow a similar route. Students need to be persuaded that the search for meaning starts with their own feelings and experiences. They need help to chart and explore those beginnings and then to "step-back" and analyze them. They need to see the study of literature as an opportunity to learn more about themselves and the world around them. The study of literature has often been considered an end in itself; we need to convince our students that it's actually a powerful and liberating "means". At the heart of that understanding lies the concept of *personal response*.

Cueing personal responses to independent reading

Independent learners have little difficulty deciding themselves how best to respond to materials and ideas in a personally significant and satisfying manner; they merely need the opportunity. Most students, however, tend to see the function of a reading, viewing, or listening experience as matching a prescribed set of answers someone else knows to a prescribed set of questions someone else devises.

Such students may, at first, appreciate a few model or sample questions to cue their initial efforts. Gradually, these students will accept more and more responsibility for the direction of their responses as they better understand how individual a personal response necessarily needs to be.

As students become more independent and begin to accept their own autonomy in the reading process, they should be "weaned" from an unbudging reliance on a list of questions.

The following sample questions are suggestions only and are intended only for students who choose to use them.

Sample cueing questions

• As you think ahead to your next day's reading, what possible directions might the story take? How do you hope the story will unfold?

• What surprised you about the section you read today? How does this change affect what might happen next in the story?

• As you read today, what feelings did you experience in response to events or characters (e.g., irritation, wonder, disbelief, recognition, dislike), and why do you think you responded this way?

• What questions do you hope to have answered next day as you read more of this story?

- What startling/unusual/effective words, phrases, expressions, or images did you come across in your reading today that you would like to have explained or clarified? Which ones would you like to use in your own writing?

- If the setting and characters were changed to reflect your own neighborhood and friends and acquaintances, how would the events of the story also have to change and why would that be so?

- Have you ever had a dream or daydream that seemed similar to an event or theme in this book? Try to describe the dream or daydream and trace the parallels.

- After reading this far, what more do you hope to learn about what these characters plan to do, what they think, feel, believe, or what happens to them?

- Do you ever wish that your own life or the people you know were more like the ones in the story you're reading? In what ways would you like the real world to be more like the world of your book?

- With what characters do you identify most closely or feel the most sympathy? What is it about these characters that makes you feel this way?

- How much do you personally agree or disagree with the way various characters think and act and the kinds of beliefs and values they hold? Where do you differ and why?

- What issues in this story are similar to real-life issues that you've thought about or had some kind of experience with? How has the story clarified or confused or changed your views on any of these issues?

- What characters and situations in the story remind you of people and situations in your own life? How are they similar and how do they differ?

- How did the characters or events in this book remind you of characters or events in other books you've read or movies or television shows you've seen? Do you prefer one of these treatments over the others? If so, why?

Responding to Independent Reading

Directions

As you read, you think about what's happening in your book in many different ways. Sometimes, questions come to your mind about some of the characters and how they are behaving. At other times, you might be impressed by the way someone or something was described. You might even be reminded of something similar that happened to you or to someone you know.

After reading independently today, try to describe the kinds of impressions and/or questions that your reading has inspired. Some people have found the following kinds of questions useful in guiding their responses. They are only suggestions. Please respond to your reading as you see fit.

- After reading this far, what more do you hope to learn about what these characters plan to do, what they think, feel, and believe, or what happens to them?

- As you think ahead to your next day's reading, what possible directions might the story take? How do you hope the story will unfold?

- If the setting and characters were changed to reflect your own neighborhood and friends and acquaintances, how would the events of the story have to change and why would that be so?

- Do you wish that your own life or the people you know were more like the ones in the story you're reading? In what ways would you like the real world to be more like the world of your book?

Focussing your students

Too many choices are often as bad as too few. This long list of cueing questions would be confusing for someone just starting in on the whole idea of personal response. The **Directions to Students** and the abbreviated list of cueing questions on page 14 will introduce students to the concept in a more focussed manner.

As the copyright notice at the bottom of the page indicates, the entire page may be reproduced for classroom use.

In the following response, Terry "feels" his way through to an understanding of the way authors use real objects to represent something more than the objects themselves. With this kind of groundwork already done, the teacher can easily and naturally extend the concept of symbolism.

Sample response to an independent reading selection

Taming the Star Runner, by S.E. Hinton,   April 17
novel; pages 50-72

A lot of odd things about reading this book. I finished reading _The Outsiders_ last week and I find out that this new one is the first Hinton book in 10 years! Then I find out she's a she. Would I have started any of these books if "Sue Hinton" were on the covers or if all her main characters were girls? Maybe that's the point. But why does she write about boys all the time? Wouldn't she know more about how girls grow up?

When Travis got involved with horses today it felt familiar and important and exciting all at the same time. Especially with "Ponyboy" from _The Outsiders_ being a writer, too, and not having a regular family. Sometimes, I think a writer just throws in a lot of stuff just because she (or he!) grew up that way. But I never had a horse or even touched one and they seem so strong and big and   beautiful.

The people in Hinton's books seem to be able to love horses

15

a lot easier than they can other people. Of course people seem to love cats and dogs a lot, too. Horses are a lot simpler than people and more natural. The outdoors seems to be better than cities, too. People seem to need to get away to get straightened out. Like "Ponyboy" and the sunset.

Anyway, Travis has got love and horses and writing all mixed up in his head and now it looks like he's going out on a drunk. And I don't see the connection because he just got great news. I stopped reading today feeling uneasy. That's a strange way to feel with a book.

- Terry (age 14)

Responding to readalouds

Students of all ages, from kindergarten through secondary school, should be read to regularly, if not daily. When setting priorities, teachers need to establish readaloud times as essential components of their program. People who are read to are more apt to read and more apt to enjoy reading enough to become life-long readers.

Written language is not the same as spoken language. We learn what the special language of books is all about by listening to books read aloud. At any age, by listening to the compelling and intricate language of literature, often more difficult than we ourselves read, we develop an understanding of the rich and complex context within which our own reading expands and flourishes.

By the same token, expository material which attempts to persuade or inform has its own individual language context directly related to the purpose for the writing. Since many teachers neglect exposition in their readaloud selections, we shouldn't be surprised when students have more difficulty reading and writing exposition than fiction. Part of the difficulty is that many content-related texts are poorly written. On the other hand, exposure has an impact. If we expect students to devote much of their in-school time reading and writing exposition, we need to inject a significant amount of expository material into our readaloud programs.

Whatever the genre, teachers should continue to choose material to read aloud which they personally believe is noteworthy. The material might be a personal favorite, a well-written account of a controversial issue, or a "classic" piece of literature. Whatever it is, a specific purpose in reading the material aloud is the first step. Obviously, the next step is for teachers to be so familiar with the material that they feel comfortable "performing" it.

With fiction, teachers often include poetry, short stories, and either excerpts from novels or a "sure-fire" novel in instalments. (Selection when using a single novel is crucial; a good rule is to choose a novel the reader can't wait to open each day. After a few sessions, if students don't feel the same, it's time to choose another.) Some teachers have had great success with picture books for older students. Picture books such as *Piggybook* by Anthony Browne, *The Mirrorstone* by Palin, Lee, and Seymour, or *The Mysteries of Harris Burdick* by Chris Van Allsburg are actually meant for older students.

With non-fiction, teachers can include newspaper and magazine articles and columns, expository material related to issues under discussion or study, and collections of contemporary and time-proven essays on a variety of themes. Items that strike a teacher's own interests or intrigue or compel are always best. If a teacher reads a hoary "chestnut" out of a sense of duty, the lack of involvement will show.

Whatever the selection, many teachers ask for a written response only when they have a specific reason for doing so and only when the material lends itself to that kind of activity. Some days, teacher and students just share a "Wow!" after the reading and move on; anything else would be anti-climactic. Other days, the reading might stimulate some small-group discussion. Too much writing can strangle a readaloud program.

After each readaloud, however, by jotting down the date and title of the readaloud selection in their response journals, students can painlessly maintain the "tracking" function. As well, if teachers are just getting started with response journals and want students to begin interacting with readalouds in a spontaneous and personally relevant manner, they might try the introduction on page 18.

As with independent reading, teachers can explain what they're looking for in the way of response and help cue the responses of those who need more support.

Responding to a Readaloud

Directions

When we listen to someone real aloud, our minds can be activated on a variety of levels. As we listen, we often jump quickly from idea to idea, image to image, and memory to memory. Sometimes, whatever we're thinking has been clearly stimulated by the reading. At other times, the link between what we're thinking and what we're listening to isn't immediately apparent.

After listening to this selection, try to describe what was happening in your mind as you listened. Sometimes, you might be reminded of a similar, real, or imagined incident; at other times, you might be especially impressed by the sound of the language or the feeling you get from a particular phrase. In reflecting on this selection, the place to start is your own personal reaction and how and why your mind reacted the way it did.

Some people have found the following kinds of questions useful in guiding their responses. These are only suggestions. Your own response may not be covered by these questions.

As you listened:

• What was happening in your mind?

> What were you thinking about?
> What images, feelings, or memories did the reading stimulate?
> What links can you trace between the reading and your thoughts?

• What was there about the reading that involved you the most?

> How were you interested or disappointed or surprised by what was read?

• What questions/comments come to mind?

> What springs to your mind that you want to ask about or say? Don't worry about how "important" the detail or issue may be; if it's on your mind, it's important enough.

Raymond Souster's poem "The Twenty-Fifth of December" is a raw, ironic, and powerful commentary on the commercialization of Christmas. In the sample response, Harriet reveals some ambivalence toward the poem and, inadvertently, her own ambivalence toward Christmas.

Sample response to a readaloud

"The Twenty-Fifth of December",   *December 14*
Poem by Raymond Souster

"Merry Christmas, suckers!" is a pretty brutal way to end a poem. Sure it was funny and all with all the price tags and slogans mixed up with the references to the commercialism of Christmas and I was laughing too. But it didn't feel right to be saying all those things about such a special time! You wouldn't want little kids reading a poem like that 'cause it would spoil all the fun and the magic of Santa Claus and presents and the tree and candy and all.

     We have good times around Christmas. Sure it gets lonely sometimes. I read once that there are more suicides around Christmas than any other time and I can believe it. It must be hard if you're alone or poor or sick. I wonder how many people there are like that? Regular people get uptight too. They start rushing around buying all their presents and they're so busy that they don't have time to have fun with their kids or their friends or anything. Then it gets to be one big drunk. But I sure wouldn't mind owning a toy store!

                           - Harriet M. (age 14)

If you've ever wondered about the value of picture books to older students, notice how Anthony Browne's *Piggybook* stimulates a highly sophisticated, philosophical "inner dialogue" in the following response by a sixteen-year-old student.

Sample response to a picture book

Piggybook, by Anthony Browne   May 17
A picture book

When I realized that everything in the house was becoming pig-like a little lightbulb clicked on over my head. After the mother/wife left the house, whatever was inside the husband and children became more and more visible. Their physical transformation indicated the deep-rooted selfish, sexist, and mindless attitudes they had been carrying around inside.

Then I saw the wallpaper turn from flowers to pigs' heads and pigs' snouts and heads appeared everywhere from the doorknobs to the salt shaker. And then I started to wonder about how much we all turn the world into a reflection of what we are inside. Is the glass half-full or half-empty? But, if you're mean inside do you turn the world mean? Or does a mean world turn you mean? What about rose-colored glasses? Is it bad to live in a rosy world?

It's not as if we all can't agree that a door is a door. What I never really thought about before was how different we all feel about that door. Are we afraid of what's behind it? Anxious to open it? Is it locked all the time? It's like ten painters all painting the same scene and coming up with ten totally different versions of the same thing. Which is the real one? The one you painted or the one I painted?

- Raymond J. (age 16)

Although Corrine doesn't like the singer or the song, she's able to "pick" her way through to a good understanding of some of the imagery and the intent behind the song. With little personal knowledge of the issues presented or formal, critical language, she has started to unlock meaning from a complex poem.

Sample response to a song

"First We Take Manhattan",   February 14
A song by Leonard Cohen

As a singer Leonard Cohen makes a pretty good poet. This isn't my kind of music; I didn't even like the version with Jennifer Warnes. His version is really different, too. Maybe that's what kind of sticks in my mind. He sounds so evil in this song. Of course that sort of fits in with what he's talking about. But that's not too clear either. All this stuff about the bad things in Manhattan and how they're going to "take" it (whoever "they" are).

Why Berlin? You know it sounds like the second world war and the Nazis. The Nazis aren't in Manhattan. They aren't even in Berlin anymore! I guess evil is, though. But Cohen sure makes it sound like us and them. I just remembered the beginning when someone was speaking German like over an intercom or something. Who are the Nazis now if they aren't the Nazis?

The other thing that I remembered is the gift he gets of a monkey and a plywood violin. He practises with them until he's ready. Now I know this guy's a poet and he means something but none of my friends would know what that's all about. It sounds cheap and weird and kind of crazy. Maybe if I saw the video it would help. I can't remember the Jennifer Warnes video. Very strange.

- Corrinne M. (age 12)

3 ∗ Responding to media

Personal response lies at the heart of media literacy. In its positive form, a response to a media experience can touch a person emotionally and intellectually, stimulate reflection, and encourage inner change. When we share an artist's vision, we can use that vision to illuminate, reassess, and possibly redirect what we believe, what we value, and how we conduct our lives.

The negative aspect of a personal response to media stems from the potential of media to reconstruct our vision of reality. Especially with films, television, videotape, and electronic and print advertising, the image seems so "real" that we accept the persuasive or attractive or powerful image as "truth." If that "truth" is riddled with a variety of stereotypes or with an unbalanced or extreme view of sexuality or violence, then the image tends to reinforce our own negative values.

Some people see that link as a reason for censorship; unfortunately, they fail to recognize that the values run both ways. As we've learned with reading print, words on a page have no absolute meaning. Comprehension occurs in the mind and is directly affected by an individual's experiences. Our comprehension of media operates the same way. Depending on past experiences and the beliefs and values developed from those experiences, two people can witness the same image and come away with two, totally different perceptions.

The screen may present a stereotype, for example; the viewer may even recognize how and why the stereotype was created. Whether the viewer "sees" that stereotype as "good" or "bad" depends not on the screen image but rather on a viewer's personal value system. Whether or not the screen displays a stereotype, that viewer's mind continues to "see" stereotypes in real life. Since the process is reciprocal, the place to start is with the individual, not the image. Burying a negative value doesn't change it; eventually it rises again.

For change to occur, the first need is to identify what an individual perceives and the value system influencing that perception. Only then can we help the individual to understand why the experience is perceived in that way and to test those values in a variety of contexts. Developing personal response to media is crucial to the process of uncovering and coming to terms with our operational values.

The process of recording their responses to a wide range of media experiences will help students, first, to codify them and, later, facilitate analysis and understanding.

Cueing personal response to media

Have you ever watched a commercial on television and wondered how such a bland or bizarre or transparent image could possibly be effective? More likely than not the message wasn't meant for you. When exploring students' personal responses to media, start with the media and the messages they're interested in and to which they are exposed and susceptible. A first step could be a simple survey. The following questions would serve that purpose.

• What television programs do you watch most often?

• What are your favorite films?

• What rock videos do you like best?

• What print and electronic advertising is directed toward your age group?

• What radio stations do you listen to?

Next, devise as many in-class opportunities as possible for them to view, respond to, and discuss each type of experience. Keep in mind that, although some techniques are common from one medium to another, each medium is a separate entity with a separate "language" and a separate set of "rules" governing its operation.

Students can become confused with lists of media techniques and technical jargon; the form can easily overwhelm the function. An awareness of technique should unfold gradually. As with any worthwhile and important process, it takes time.

Responding to film

A personal response to a film often operates in a different manner from a response to a print experience. Film is a mixture of sound, motion, and picture. The "reality" of the film is so vividly and fully realized that the mind becomes involved in vicariously living that reality and less consciously reflective of the experience.

Upon immediate reflection, many students feel that "it was what it was." They liked it or they didn't like it; they liked some of the characters or they didn't. Usually they have a difficult time removing themselves from the film in an objective way. Since a film is often a less obvious "construction" than a novel or a music video, it's easier to accept an impression rather than probe the feelings behind that impression. In a sense, the experience is too "real" to analyze or question.

(See the **Directions to Students** and the sample student response to film on pages 26-28.)

Responding to a Film

Part 1

Directions

Don't worry about retelling the story of the film or even talking about whether the film was "good" or "bad." Try, instead, to think about you and your life in connection with the film and the characters in it.

- What connections are you thinking about?

- What personal feelings or memories are surfacing?

- What seems important about the film that you want to say?

If what you want to say about the film isn't clear, try reflecting on some of the following questions. Remember that these are only suggestions.

- When you think about this film, what first comes to your mind? Is there an image or character or situation that you start to think about?

- Do you start with a gesture someone made or a dominant color you noticed, a controversial issue, or, perhaps, something that confused you? Where do these thoughts lead?

Responding to a Film

Part 2

Directions

- What startling/unsettling/vivid images seem to stick in your mind?

  What is it that you remember about these images or the way they were presented?

  How do they seem to tie in with the experiences or feelings you've had in real life?

- When you think about this film, is there a character, a situation or an issue which you immediately compare with a person (even yourself) or a situation or an issue you know personally? How do they compare?

  How does the real-life experience affect what you think about the screen experience?

  How does the screen experience affect your understanding of the real-life experience?

- Do you wish your own life or the people you know were more like the world of the film and the characters in that world?

  Did you identify with one character more than any other?

  How much did you agree or disagree with the people in the film, the way they behaved, or the kinds of values and beliefs they displayed?

Prior to a unit on print advertising, the teacher showed a film on the image of women in advertising. The intent was to help students get beyond the surface impact of ads and begin to appreciate the deliberate constructions. In the process, the teacher hoped to provide them with some of the visual language of ads and stimulate discussion of stereotyping and imbedded values. As the following response indicates, the film offers some powerful and provocative images. *

Sample response to a film

Still Killing Us Softly   *October 21*
Documentary Film

It's hard not to feel angry and kind of sick when you see how women are trapped in this image and everyone thinks it's just fine. So maybe there are two sides and guys are trapped in this macho thing too. But they aren't packaged up and told that growing old is bad and how dumb they are and treated like an idiot toy and turned against each other. But what's frightening is that it all happens so naturally and it all seems so right. You see the ads and the tv commercials and you know that it's all around you all the time. And everybody talks about how sexism is so bad and your parents and your teachers and the government tell you you can be anything you want but do you see women as principals much or as heads of companies or in the government? The worst thing is that if you don't want to be a house-keeper or a baby machine you have to turn into a man to get ahead in the business world! How do you get people to change? You look at the television programs and rock videos and you know that no matter what some people are saying nothing is really

* *Still Killing Us Softly: Advertising's Image of Women*, Cambridge
Documentary Films, P.O. 385, Cambridge, Mass., 02139. 1988.

different. Maybe it's even more frightening. People want us to believe that there is no longer a problem. Well, guess again! Open a magazine. Turn on the tv. Talk to your boy friend.

- Wanda K. (age 15)

Responding to television

The statistics derived from television's looming presence have become almost commonplace. We're no longer shocked by the fact that high school graduates have spent less time in school than watching television, or that they've been exposed to hundreds of hours of television commercials. In spite of this "electronic" fact of life, however, we remain unsure of the impact this kind of exposure is having on our students' value systems, or even our own.

How much of what our students see on television do they accept as "real" and how able are they to "see through" what they see? From the cartoon-like stereotypes of "sit-coms" to the glossy and romanticized violence of crime shows, television presents an endless barrage of aberrated images. When a rapid-fire, highly edited, and carefully-managed newscast is blithely accepted as a realistic portrayal of day-to-day events, where do students draw the line?

The main difficulty in dealing with television programming in schools is the lack of immediacy. We want our students to develop an interactive relationship with a medium that appears temptingly benign and passive. Except for educational programming, however, their viewing habits are developed and maintained in their homes. To bridge the actual experience of viewing and the processing of that experience through discussion and reflection, students need to become aware of and examine their personal relationship with television. Through the response journal, students can examine what they have been watching, how they're being touched by what they watch, what kind of sense they're making of television, and why they continue to watch.

Before getting to the personal response stage, however, teacher and students need a clear picture of what everyone is watching and how often. Students need to become aware of their own viewing habits and those of their friends. The survey **Who's Watching What?** begins the process. (The teacher should also complete the survey.) The teacher gathers the individual figures and computes a class average for each type of programming.

(See the chart **Developing a Viewer Profile** and the **Directions to Students** on pages 32-33.)

Responding to "Soaps" and "Sit-Coms"

Two of the most popular types of programs on television use an exaggerated and distorted form of reality to great effect. Both count on developing loyal fans who will watch their programs regularly over a long period of time. Both hold the potential for bending our expectations for the lives we actually lead.

With daytime "soaps", action is slowed down to such an extent that events seem to unfold at the same rate they do in real life. A crisis, for example, drags on over a number of episodes, and characters agonize over each developing detail much as "real" people might. Small wonder that with action at a minimum and crisis at the maximum the world of soaps is "awash" with emotions.

In this highly-charged, emotional context, the pull to identify with the physically attractive and primarily youthful characters is strong and insidious. The combination of these attractive, romantic figures struggling day-by-day through every gritty, seamy, or difficult situation that human beings can encounter is irresistible.

Add the "lifestyles of the rich and famous" and you find the same formula repeated in nighttime "soaps". Regardless of our socio-economic status, since their emotions are just like ours, we can identify with the rich and powerful. For good or bad, the bridge between their world and ours is easily negotiated. We recognize, we identify, and we're moved.

With "sit-coms" (situation comedies), the context comes first. Regardless of stereotypical characters and their often bizarre behavior, we can validate their long-term relationships and the familiar and predictable problems they encounter. In spite of the fact that the characters themselves, their reactions, and their approaches to the resolution of conflict are exaggerated, over-simplified, and frequently irrational, we recognize, we identify, and we laugh.

The temptation with these programs, as with so much of television, is the vivid, immediate sense of "peering in" at a parallel world. The danger is that we accept the concerns, attitudes, aspirations, and values we see there as real. If students see television as a "window" into the functioning of the actual world or as a standard against which to judge their own lives, they can only remain confused and unhappy.

By recording their personal responses in a journal, students can begin to crystalize and articulate what kind of sense they're making of these television "realities" and why they're making that kind of "sense".

After the students fill out the **Developing a Viewer Profile** chart individually, the teacher gathers the data from the class and works out an average frequency count for each category. The students add this information to their own charts and then use the **Responding to the Viewer Profile** sheet that follows this chart.

Developing a Viewer Profile

Who's Watching What?

Directions

This survey will help you examine your viewing habits over a seven-day period. Think back over the last week or over a "typical" viewing week and decide how often you watch the following types of programs. If you watch a particular kind of show every day for seven days, give it a frequency count of "7". (If you watch that type of program more than once a day, still just count it as "once".) If you don't watch a particular kind of show at all, give that category "0". Count only the viewing you do outside of school.

Type of Programming	My Count for a Week	Average Count from the Class
Children's Shows		
Cartoons		
Variety Shows		
Game Shows		
Talk Shows		
"Sit-Coms"		
Sports		
Daytime "Soaps"		
Crime/Adventure		
Hospital/Legal		
Fantasy/Sci-Fi		
News/Documentaries/ Public Affairs		
TV Movies		
Movies on Video		
MTV		
Other?		

Responding to the Viewer Profile

Directions

The viewing survey provides you with a profile of your viewing habits and the viewing habits of those in your class. In your journal, comment on your viewing habits, how you normally regard yourself as a TV watcher, or the impressions you gained from the profile. The following questions may serve as a springboard into your feelings on the matter.

• What picture emerges from the survey of you as a television watcher?

  How does this picture compare with how you regard yourself?

  What aspects of your viewing habits surprise you or make you feel uneasy or embarrassed? Why?

• How does your own profile compare with that of the class average?

  How are your habits different?

  How do you feel about these differences and why do you feel that way?

• What impressed you about the results or seemed especially significant?

• What more would you like to know about your own viewing habits or those of your friends?

Responding to "Soaps" and "Sit-Coms"

Directions

Think of your favorite "soaps" or "sit-coms" (or the ones you watch the most). Week after week, certain features about the shows attract you. Sometimes, memorable episodes dealing with a specific issue in a particular way will create a special attraction for you. Probably for a combination of reasons, the characters and situations have gained your attention and will continue to do so.

When you consider these programs in general and certain favorite episodes, what thoughts and feelings arise immediately and remain uppermost in your mind? If you have difficulty unravelling these thoughts and feelings, some of the following questions may trigger a significant response.

• How do you explain your attraction and loyalty to a particular show?

  What strong opinions or reactions have been stirred up in you by what the characters do or say?

• With whom do you identify most closely on this particular show? Least?

  How are these people like or unlike you or who you want to be?

  How do these characters compare with the people you meet every day?

• If you could switch characters from the show with real people, who would you switch and which way?

  Why would you make these switches?

  How would real life be affected by these changes?

  How would the world of the television show be changed?

Responding to rock videos

The world of music videos is a rich source of material for personal response. Keep in mind that many students already know more about this medium than you do. With exposure to rock videos, they've become accustomed to mixtures of fantasy and "reality", special effects of all kinds, role-playing, surreal imagery, and the value systems imbedded in specific types of music.

Some videos, "heavy metal" for example, often project images that are blatantly sexist, sexual, and violent. The characters in such videos are portrayed as worldly, daring, rebellious, and exciting wanderers. Other sub-groups, such as "rap", "soul", or "country", have their own "looks." Many of your students are familiar with these "traditions", are fans of a particular genre, and expect to see the characteristics of each type maintained.

Middle-of-the-road music produces more variety in the approach to videos. Don't assume, however, that everyone likes a video simply because it's on the charts. A survey once revealed that Michael Jackson was the most liked and the most disliked artist in North America - at the same time!

(See the **Directions to Students** on page 36.)

Responding to a Rock Video

Directions

After looking at a particular video, try to describe the impression it had on you, the kinds of thoughts and feelings you have about it, the aspects of the video you remember most, or simply a feature of your own life you started to think about in conjunction with the video. Some students have found the following questions useful. They are only suggestions. Try to respond spontaneously about the things you feel are important or noteworthy.

• What images or brief scenes seemed most vivid? What phrases or repeated words appealed to you? What actions, gestures, aspects of clothing, or similar "small moments" seem to "stick" in your mind?

• As the video played, could you feel yourself amused, attracted, repelled, excited, disgusted, or irritated by any of the sequences? What was depicted as "good"? What was depicted as "bad"? Could you "see" yourself as anyone in the video or as a part of the world portrayed?

• As you watched the video, did your mind start making connections with scenes in other videos, or real-life episodes or memories? What connections were you making? How were you reacting?

• What kind of music video usually appeals to you? How does whether or not you like the music affect whether or not you like the video? Does it ever work the other way around? Do you like a video to tell a song's story exactly or do you enjoy unusual effects? What kinds of scenes or effects or situations do you usually like in a video?

Responding to print advertising

For this activity, ask your students to collect five or six print advertisements from magazines and newspapers they have been reading. Some samples should be in color.

Try to focus your students before they begin. Remind them that when we look at ads, our minds are active on a variety of levels. Although we are not consciously aware of what's happening, our eyes quickly dart from feature to feature all over the page. In that same split second, our minds are interconnecting colors with feelings with images with feelings with memories with feelings, and so on. Trying to trace those connections is next to impossible. If we are part of the group targetted for that ad, however, we are "supposed" to feel a certain way about it. Remind them that feeling is the place to start.

Then ask them to look over the ads they have collected, thinking only of how they "feel" about them. They would then choose the one that is most appealing, intriguing, or powerful and respond following the **Directions to Students** on page 38.

Responding to Print Advertising

Directions

As you look more closely at the advertisement you've chosen, try to describe the kind of impression you've formed of it, the features you notice, or the thoughts or memories or emotions connected with it that you can identify.

What do you notice about how your mind is reacting? Some students have found the following kinds of questions useful in guiding their responses. They are only suggestions. Follow and trust your own reactions, thoughts, and feelings.

- Don't try to "understand" the ad. Let your eyes rest on the page. Be aware of colors, patterns, shapes, images, words or phrases, and the total "look." What aspects of the ad seem to draw your attention? How do they make you feel?

- What connections do you start to make between the ad and your own life, the way it is now or the way you would like it to be? How does the ad seem to stimulate your dreams, your desires, or your fears?

- What flashes of memory surface as you consider the ad? What feelings (embarrassment, humiliation, excitement, guilt, fear, etc.) are identified with these episodes? How did the ad make these memories surface?

- Try to enter the "world" of the advertisement. If that world were merged with your own, what parts of the "advertisement world" would have to change in order to become "real" and truly fit in with your life? What aspects of your life could realistically change to become more like the world of the ad?

Barbette responded to a Coty advertisement for "Coty Wild Musk and Coty Musk for Men". Under a large, bold-face title, "The Wild Ones", two young adults stare out of the ad with brooding, almost surly expressions on their faces. The young male is dressed in jeans and a black t-shirt and is sitting half in and half out of the open trunk of a sports car. His arms embrace a young female, standing, leaning in toward him. School books have been tossed on the ground and litter the shadowed area under the car. The couple seems to be in a parking lot, possibly a school lot. The copy in small print accompanying a picture of the product at the base of the ad says, "How did we find each other? The attraction was irresistible. The fragrance-natural and untamed. Coty Wild Musk & Coty Musk for Men. And nobody but us has to understand it."

Barbette's response clearly illustrates how she was able to follow the personal response instructions and let her feelings lead her to an understanding of how the ad was operating.

Sample response to print advertising

Coty Perfume Magazine Ad   *June 20*

They were looking straight at me and the title "Wild Ones" and they seemed so tough and apart from everyone else and everything else except they were together. I guess I kept looking back and forth from their faces and cold and distant eyes and back to the title. You can tell they're together and in love but even though they're close and touching it's not sexy except for the fact that you know they'll do anything they want whenever they want. Actually, sitting in the trunk of the car is kind of sexy and her hair makes her look like she's free and wild. The funny thing is I kind of had to force myself to look down and see what they were selling because their eyes were so attracting and then I saw what it was and it seemed like a strange thing to be selling in a girl's magazine. After a minute or two I noticed the school books dumped on the ground and that really fits in with being

*wild and free and doing what you want whenever you want
and just daring someone to stop you. I'd really like to find
out what it smells like. I guess that's the whole point isn't it?*

- Barbette (age 16)

Responding to newspapers and magazines

Newspapers and magazines of all types can and should be brought into the classroom for reading and study. Special attention should be paid to the ones that students actually read, the sections they favor, and the issues and stories that attract them most. Eventually, in any long-term and comprehensive media literacy unit, students will learn how and why to discriminate among newspapers and magazines. The first step in this process is to help them reflect on what they're reading and why.

For the following activity, students should have both newspapers and magazines and the time to flip through them and read whatever attracts them. Ideally, a variety of material should be available to satisfy whatever style of reporting individuals prefer. Most teachers prefer to separate the study of the newspaper from that of the magazine.

(See the **Directions to Students** on page 41.)

Responding to Newspapers

Directions

Read through the newspaper. When you're finished, think about how you went about reading the paper, what you read and what you didn't, and how you were attracted or repelled by what you found. As you frame your responses, some of the following questions may prove helpful.

• What issues or types of stories seemed to draw you to them?

When did you feel impatient, amused, frustrated, irritated, angry, disbelieving, or moved, and why did you feel that way?

• What sections did you read and which ones did you skip over?

What ads, types of stories, photos, headlines, or other features grabbed your attention?

What did you actually find compared with what you expected to find?

What interests/attitudes/feelings seemed to surface regularly as you flipped through the paper?

• What sections/articles/ads seemed to be written with you or someone like you in mind? Which ones seemed to be meant for a different audience? How could you tell?

How was the material highlighted or presented to appeal to a particular group or to highlight a particular point of view?

• Was anything unfair in what you read? If there was, why did you feel that way about it?

Sample response to a newspaper article

The following response entry comes from the scrapbook of a Grade 9 history student. The teacher has the students clip from different issues of a newspaper five articles per month, tape or paste them into a scrapbook, and write a short summary and response — "I think this is important because…" Spelling and/or grammatical errors are not corrected or marked and do not affect the evaluation. The objective is to have students develop the habit of looking at newspapers regularly and thinking about what they read. The main criterion for evaluation, therefore, is completion of task and a mark out of 10 or 20 would be determined primarily on that basis.

Band of "Santas" swoops on war toys

By Jane Armstrong Toronto Star

The mission of the Santas was simple: strip the "war toys" from a North York store and put candy canes in their place.

But Metro police scrooged the operation yesterday and charged the bearded band of protesters, each dressed up as Santa Claus, with trespassing.

Six Santas and two elves were handed $53.75 fines following the aborted protest.

The Santas, none of whom would reveal their real names, descended on Toy City on Dufferin St. at 2 p.m.

Demonstrators chanted anti-war-toy slogans outside the department store while the Santas and elves headed for the shelves.

When frantic sales clerks tried to stop the interlopers, they started singing songs, refusing to budge.

'War isn't a game'

The trespassers said they hailed from the North Pole, but the pamphlets they handed out were compiled by the Alliance for Non-Violent Action, a group opposed to the sale of toys that promote violence.

A bearded protester said the group sent letters to every toy store in Toronto asking them to remove such toys from their shelves.

"In this store alone, I've seen a serrated Rambo knife, something called a Super Stilleto Scorpion and a plastic rocket launcher," a female Santa said.

"We want people to know that war isn't a game and Christmas is a time for peace," she told store manager Mario Addesa, 24.

Addesa begged the red-suited intruders to leave, arguing that customers have a right to choose what gifts they buy their children.

Seven police officers from 32 Division arrived shortly afterward and escorted all the Santas and their elves out of the store.

Police said no merchandise was taken out of the store.

The Toronto Star, December 9, 1988

Band of "Santas" swoops on war toys

A group of "Santas" invaded the Toy City on Dufferin Street in North York at 2: p.m. this afternoon. They were after the war toys. They (men and women) belong to an organization opposed to the sale of toys that promote violence. All of the Santas and two elves were charged with trespassing. The Santas would not reveal their names.

Standing outside of the store were demonstrators chanting slogans of anti-war toys. The Santas' mission was to simply remove all of the war toys from the shelves and replace them with Christmas candy canes. This is what one of the Santas said: "In this store alone, I've seen a serrated Rambo knife, something called a Super Stilleto Scorpion and a plastic rocket launcher."

I think that it's important for people to know that some people are opposed to the sale of war toys, especially at Christmas time. There is enough violence today in the adult world. We don't need to start young kids off with serrated Rambo knives and rocket launchers. Other gifts would be more suitable at Christmas. After all, Christmas is supposed to be a time to celebrate peace, not practise war.

- Vicky (age 14)

4 * Guiding the student/teacher conference

A conference will always work best when it's a collaborative effort between you and the student. In the following suggestions, the student and the teacher share the responsibility for making the conference purposeful and productive.

Some teachers like to build as much flexibility into their conferences as possible. Rather than scheduling a separate reading and writing conference, they designate the time for a reading/writing conference. In this way, the purpose for the conference can be adapted to suit a student's needs and work pattern.

When the conference, or part of it, is focussed on the response journal, try to incorporate the following suggestions into your planning.

Purpose

Build in continuity by starting with a review of the last conference and following up on any outstanding questions, tasks, or contracts arising from that conference.

Deal with the student's agenda next. A student might have a question arising from his/her independent reading, a problem encountered in a small-group discussion, or any number of other concerns. If you demonstrate that you respect and value the student's agenda, he/she will develop self-direction and that agenda will grow and flourish.

With your own agenda, maintain your objectivity and keep value judgments to a minimum. The conference should be an exchange of views and a problem-solving discussion, not a "third-degree."

If it's an observation you've made on a small-group discussion you've monitored, explain what you saw or heard, why you felt it was noteworthy, and ask the student to put it into a larger context for you. For example, you may be concerned about the small amount of material being read. If you start the conference by advising the student that he/she is not reading enough, you immediately set up an adversarial tone and effectively short-circuit the problem-solving potential of the conference. Instead, ask the student to describe how much he/she is reading, how this amount compares with the student's normal rate, any difficulties the student may be encountering with the material, or personal preoccupations the individual may be experiencing.

Depending on what you discover, you may feel the effort is adequate or you may want to establish a contract with the student to increase the amount read. If so, make sure you have the student set a realistic goal over a reasonably short period of time, and decide how and when the contract will be reviewed. (A sample reading/writing contract is provided on page 50.)

Record-keeping

At the very least, both you and the student should record that the conference took place on a specific date. The student should note this and any other information related to the conference in his/her response journal.

Any other record-keeping should be purposeful. For example, if you and the student agree to meet in two days' time, both of you should make a note of it. If you've given the student a specific task or suggestion, ask the student to jot it down. If you're going to try to locate a specific book for a student, write down the title in your records.

The conference itself should not be evaluated. If agreement is reached on an issue, however, or an unusual observation comes out of the conference, these kinds of details should be noted. You would definitely want to record the fact that you and the student had agreed that he/she should try to read more and the steps to be taken to achieve that goal. By the same token, if a student makes a shrewd analogy during the conference, revealing a new interest, a sudden insight, or a lot of extra-curricular reading, you'd want to note those observations.

The record-keeping should hold no secrets or surprises for anyone. The student should always know what you are recording, why you are recording that information, and how it might enter into his/her evaluation.

For record purposes one page per student is convenient and workable. Any less and you wouldn't have enough space to make your notes; any more and you might try to say too much and get lost in the paperwork. Keep the pages in a small, loose-leaf binder. The pads of small, "stick-on" message paper are a handy way of recording observations between conferences. Just write the observation, date it, and stick it on the student's page. When the conference comes up, you can discuss the observation with the student and, if appropriate, make a permanent record of it.

Reflective thinking

As a record of a process over time, the response journal supplies you with a number of checkpoints in a variety of areas. By linking a specific set of checkpoints, you and the student can discuss the profile that takes shape. For example, you may have noted a reluctance on the part of a student to initiate ideas in small-group discussions. By mentioning this observation and checking through the response journal records of small-group discussions, you and the student can place the observation in a context over time and assess its validity.

Similarly, patterns revealed in the response journals need to be identified, discussed, and evaluated. Students need to be encouraged to take over this function on their own and make it a prime objective. Growth in self-evaluation and independence in learning go hand in hand with and develop out of reflection.

Real questions

Many books on writing and reading conferences contain lists of the kinds of questions you should be asking. Actually, you are already perfectly capable of asking any question you need to ask. The key is to make sure you really want to find out the answer.

Try not to ask questions to which you already know the answers. Through so much exposure to these kinds of questions over the years, students instantly realize that these questions signal a "test." Why else would someone ask a question when he or she already knows the answer? The student, then, tries to guess the "right" answer in your mind. When you start asking questions like that, the collaborative, problem-solving tone of the conference is lost.

Instead, try to respond to the student as you would to a peer. If you're confused, say so. Then ask whatever questions are necessary to clear up the confusion. If you think something may be bothering the student, say so. Explain why you think that way and ask the student to clarify the situation for you. If you have a reason to probe, probe. If you have nothing to say, the conference is over.

Teachers often fall into the habit of asking students to "tell" them about the latest book they have read. A long and tedious retelling usually follows. Why not pursue a more interesting line? If it's science fiction, find out if you and the student have read some of the same books or watched similar science fiction films or television shows. Then explore your common experiences and see how the new book fits in.

Try to get students to place specific experiences into a larger context, synthesize a variety of print and media experiences, or reflect on why and how they read the way they do. Entries in the student's response journal on readalouds or remarks and observations on small-group discussions can raise intriguing questions. The discussions should be a learning experience for both of you. Follow you own instincts, react naturally and spontaneously, and always try to hold up your end of a real discussion.

Definite time limits

Set a maximum time for each conference, let the student know, and observe the limits. If you haven't covered everything, either leave the other issues until the next time or schedule another conference. The response journals will work best if they are reviewed regularly face to face. Set a schedule and stick with it. As well, there's no minimum time. When the student's agenda and your own have been covered, the conference is over.

Sample teacher record sheet

Prior to this conference, the teacher made some observations on small pieces of "stick-on" message paper and placed them on the student's record page.

> Feb. 21 - Dave and Gary R. were arguing in discussion group; I intervened.

> Feb. 22 - Dave and Gary R. disagreed in discussion of film; I stepped in.

Notice how these and other issues were raised during the conference, often by the student, and how they were resolved. Notice, as well, how individual program planning grows out of the conference.

Response journal conference

Student's name: _David Carter_

Conference Date:	Issues Raised	Actions Taken/ Goals Set
Feb. 23	1. Dave wanted me to read aloud to the class some poems from _Class Dismissed Two_: he really likes them.	1. He's going to read some of his favorites to the class.
	2. Dave and Susan want to write an anthology of original poems together (see contract) based on _Class Dismissed Two_.	2. The project will be finished in two weeks (March 8); independent study, worth 10%.
	3. Dave's had trouble resolving differences with Gary in discussions this week. He's not sure why.	3. Must monitor the next few discussions; talk to Gary; Dave will "track" the problem in his journal responses.

Sample reading/writing contract

Date: _Feb. 23_

Student's Name: _David Carter_

Why a new goal is necessary: _Dave has proposed an independent study project with Susan Kramer to be worth 10% of their term mark._

What the new goal is: _He will write a book of poems with Susan like the ones in Class Dismissed Two. The book will be ready by March 8._

When the new goal will be reviewed: _March 8_

Student Signature: _David Carter_

Teacher Signature: _L. Parsons_

Goal Review: The goal ((was)/ was not) reached.

Student Comment: _The book turned out even better than we hoped. Writing the poems made me think about all the people I know and what different people are like._

Teacher Comment: _The poems are engaging, clever, and realistic. The partnership worked well, the product is excellent, and the project was a great success. We're going to have them typed and bound._

Student Signature: _David Carter_

Teacher Signature: _L. Parsons_

50

The following notes were prepared by a student for a student/teacher conference. Notice how the suggestions from the preceding conference were followed.

Sample of pre-conference student notes

Notes for conference: Feb. 23
Last conference: Feb. 12

Books read: <u>Dear Bruce Springsteen</u> by Kevin Major (p. 75-132)
<u>Fade</u> by Robert Cormier (up to p. 153)

Other reading: <u>Class Dismissed Two, More High School Poems,</u>
by Mel Glenn

Extended to <u>Dear Bruce Springsteen</u>   Feb. 12, 15
responses: to <u>Fade</u>   Feb. 20, 22
to <u>Class Dismissed Two</u>   Feb. 19
to group discussions   Feb. 13, 20
to readalouds   Feb. 14, 16, 20

Suggestions from last conference

- try reading some poetry; that book you suggested was great! Gave me some ideas for poems about people I know. I'm working with Susan on it.
- contract: Write at least 3 extended responses before next conference. Done!

Questions for the teacher

- I read the review of Kevin Major's new book in the newspaper. It says most of his books are banned in schools. Why are they banned? How come we're allowed to read them?
- How much do you think my journal has improved since last term? In marks, I mean?

51

Sample responses during a one-day period

The following responses were recorded to a variety of activities during the same day. Although the response to the teacher's readaloud selection and to the peer reading/writing conference with Susan are detailed and perceptive, the responses to the new novel and to the film discussion give only the date and basic data.

---

from The Moosepire by D. Pinkwater   Tues., Feb. 20
A readaloud

Well, you did warn us. I don't think anyone in class was surprised that this guy is your favorite author. He is a little weird. Now that you've read a couple of things by him, I can see he has a very special way of writing, of thinking really. He's funny but he doesn't make you burst out laughing like some writers. The scenes he creates are not like everyday life. His stories are like building blocks piled haphazardly on top of each other. They're not all that exciting, either, but they're so strange and different from everyday life that it makes you look at things in a different way and keeps you hanging on. He's not totally, wildly fantastic, either. I think I can tolerate his stories because they're about everyday things and strangeness all mixed together. But I do think it's time for a change of pace.

Fade by Robert Cormier   Tues., Feb. 20
A novel. I read pgs. 1 - 47
- just got started, read to p.47

Reading/Writing Conference   Tues., Feb. 20
with Susan C.

I showed Susan the "Class Dismissed II" poems, especially
the poems "Howie Bystrom" and "Wendy Tarloff". If you
don't know them, the "Howie" poem is about Howie getting
dumped by his girlfriend at an amusement park from
Howie's point of view and "Wendy" is the girl dumping him
from her point of view. Two poems, one situation. The poems
aren't really like poems. They're like real people and real
things that happen to them written in a very clear and
believable way. Susan and I talked it over ad we're going to
try the same thing. We made up two characters. (Actually we
didn't. She's thinking of a "real" guy and I'm thinking of a
"real" girl.) And we thought about using the whizbang ride
at the carnival down at the mall parking lot. The two people
don't know each other, sit side by side in the same car, get
shoved and bumped around and get off the ride holding
hands without ever saying a word. Susan's going to write
what was going on in the girl's head and I'm going to write
what was going on in the boy's head. We're going to work on
it tomorrow.

Still Killing Us Softly (film)   Tues., Feb. 20

- had a discussion with Marge, Bill, and Craig about the film

53

5 * Developing small-group discussions

Co-operative learning is one of the most powerful learning/teaching strategies that educators have discovered, and response journals have an important role to play in that process. Successful small-group discussions don't just happen; they develop as a result of careful planning, positive coaching, and lots of practice. By collaborating on a regular basis in pairs and in groups of three, four, or more, students can develop the interactive skills necessary to share and build on the foundation of each other's interests, backgrounds, experiences, and insights.

Small-group discussions in language arts or English classes can serve many different purposes, and response journals can help in two ways. They can be used to focus on the dynamics of a group, regardless of the content of the discussion or task. In certain circumstances, they can also allow an individual to comment on the course of group investigations into literature.

Special care is advised in using a written component to a small-group discussion. In *Making Sense of Poetry: Patterns in the Process* (CCTE, 1987), Patrick Dias makes a persuasive case for not allowing any kind of writing before, during, or after a discussion about poetry. If there is a written component based on the content of a discussion, be sure you've articulated for yourself and for your students the purpose and the value of that component. Before examining the role of response journals in developing small-group discussion skills, consider some of the **don'ts** and **do's** of recording the content of discussions about literature.

Some don'ts

- **Don't** ask students to transcribe the course of the discussion. That kind of activity is usually assigned as a test of how well students were following and contributing to the discussion. As well as undercutting and devaluing the process of the discussion, this approach forces students into needless duplication. Eventually, the attitude in the group becomes "the less we say, the less we'll have to write".

- **Don't** treat discussions as rehearsals for essay-writing. A discussion is a complete learning/teaching experience in itself. If you plan to have students write an essay after a discussion, the purpose for that discussion becomes preparation for writing. Obviously, there's nothing wrong with brainstorming, webbing, and other pre-writing activities. Just don't confuse them with personal response.

- **Don't** ask students to "report" on other students in their response journals, either in terms of what they say or how they behave in discussion groups. Co-operative learning operates on a basis of trust and respect. If a group is operating inefficiently, other techniques can be used to turn the experience into a positive learning opportunity.

Some do's

- **Do** ask students to record the date and topic of each discussion and the names of the members of their groups each time. This basic "tracking" function keeps the journal record complete and can be performed before or after a discussion.

- **Do** give students an opportunity, if they choose, to record information after a discussion for use later. They may want to record such items as titles of books, surprising or intriguing facts, a reminder to look up a disputed fact, or a sudden thought or memory stimulated by the discussion.

- **Do** encourage students to trade, read, and, with the permission of the owner, extend a small-group discussion into a "paired" dialogue by corresponding in their journals.

- **Do** use the response journal to help students develop effective small-group discussion skills.

Small-group discussion skills

To be effective and responsible members of a small-group discussion, students need to be aware of the different roles they have to play in a group and to be given opportunities to practise them. The key small-group discussion roles are *sharing with others, replying to others, leading others, supporting others,* and *evaluating in a group.* Prior to a discussion, a teacher can highlight one of these roles by giving the students a few questions which establish the criteria for the skills involved. Consider the following example.

Discussion role: Sharing with others

• Do you share with other people your opinions, feelings or special knowledge?

• Do you listen carefully to others so that what you know can be linked to what they know?

• When you give an opinion, do you offer facts and reasons to support that opinion?

After the discussion, students record in their response journals such items as whether or not they practised those skills, how well they succeeded or why they didn't, and what they would try to do in future to improve their performance in that particular response role. Remember that a student comments only on his/her performance and not on that of a peer's.

The teacher can compare each student's observations with his or her own perceptions and discuss them with the student during individual conferences. Over time, the response journal entries will present the teacher with a profile of each student's involvement in group discussions, the degree to which a student is developing self-awareness, the personal goals a student sets, and the kind of success a student is finding in this area.

Students should be briefed beforehand about the process. At designated intervals, the teacher can review this process and assign a summative mark based on stated criteria. (See the sample evaluation chart on page 67.)

Highlighting particular skills

In *Learning to Work in Groups*, Matthew Miles identifies five functions that groups perform and which each group member, at various times, needs to supply. When group members accept the responsibility for fulfilling these functions as needed, the group operates efficiently.

These discussion-group responsibilities can be isolated and highlighted for students. Some sample categories and focussing questions follow. For any single discussion, you would focus on only one of these categories. By returning to the same questions at intervals, you can invite students to reflect on their own progress as well as create a "window" on the process to assist your own evaluation.

Prior to a discussion, one or more of these response roles can be highlighted. After the discussion, students record in their response journals such items as whether or not they practised that particular skill that day, how well they succeeded or why they didn't, and what they would like to try to do in future discussions to improve their performance in that particular area.

Cueing questions for discussion roles

Sharing with others

- Do you share with other people your opinions, feelings, or special knowledge?

- Do you listen carefully to others so that what you know can be linked to what they know?

- When you give an opinion, do you offer facts and reasons to support that opinion?

Replying to others

- Do you listen carefully so that you can ask clarifying questions or offer clarifying statements when necessary?

- Do you reply freely to other people's questions, interests, problems, and concerns?

- Do you share equally in the talking the group does?

Leading others

- Do you suggest your own ideas, other ways to solve problems, or new directions for the group to explore?

- Are you able to speak up without cutting someone off or detracting from the progress the group is making?

- Are you able to offer suggestions without dominating the discussion?

Supporting others

- Do you go out of your way to help other people have their turn to speak in a group?

- Do you indicate in your gestures, facial expressions, or posture that you are interested in what is being said?

- Do you make other people still feel worthwhile, even though you disagree with their point of view?

- Do you give people credit when they deserve it, even if they disagree with you?

Evaluating in a group

- Do you indicate whether or not you agree with ideas or decisions and why you do or don't?

- Do you consider how well the group is working and how you might help the group work even better?

- Do you re-examine your own opinions and decisions and adjust them when someone comes up with a better idea?

The following response to a small-group discussion shows that the student is thinking about her role in the group, noting what aspect of her process she was trying to focus on, and evaluating her performance. This self-analysis is both thoughtful and sincere, particularly perceptive for an eleven-year-old.

Tiffany clearly illustrates the value of helping students reflect on their own learning processes. By focussing on how she learns, Tiffany can affect how well she learns. Notice, as well, that progress occurs as a process over time.

Sample response to a small-group discussion

Discussion with Barb, Jack, and   *September 30*
Karen about the poem "Flight One"

I felt more comfortable with the group today. I still have a hard time butting in when someone's talking but I don't know what else to do when we ramble on and on. I think the first thing I have to do is stop talking when I've said what I want to say. I was really trying to listen to other people today and to add things on to what they said. They really appreciated that because it wasn't all you talk, I talk, you talk, I talk. It was more like it was all mixed up and part of the same argument.

The idea of sharing went well too. When a disagreement occurred it wasn't I'm right and you're wrong. We seemed to be able to say that it's not necessary for everyone to agree or think the same. I guess it helps when there's no right answer. I mentioned yesterday that I have this habit of only talking to one person in a group and that I kept repeating ideas when I didn't know what else to say. I thought it went better today. We had a good discussion.

- Tiffany T. (age 11)

6 * Evaluating response journals

Right from the start, your students should be included in the total process of using response journals. They need to know what they are, why and how they will be used, and, most importantly, how they will be evaluated. Their own suggestions for implementing and operating the journals should also be considered. If possible, the group and/or individuals might suggest or select some of the evaluation criteria.

Be sure, as well, that whatever you want to happen in those journals is clearly articulated and that those criteria are built into the evaluation system. If your objectives are clearly stated, evaluation can direct and support the learning process. For example, if you feel that students should be looking back at past entries and reflecting on their own growth or changes in their opinions, tell them in advance that their journals need to include this kind of item. Show them the marking scheme you'll be using and indicate how long it will be before you formally evaluate their work.

Over a two- or three-week period, you can check informally or with self-evaluation checklists to see if students are, in fact, including that kind of entry in their journals and discuss with them how you view their progress (formative evaluation). After the designated period, assign a mark for the extent to which each student has met that criterion (summative evaluation). By discussing with a student how the mark was arrived at and what the student would have to do to improve the mark over the next evaluation period, you make the mark work for you in a formative manner.

Variations are possible. If you want to emphasize one specific criterion, simply weight it with more marks. As students become more adept at certain kinds of entries, you may want to stimulate other uses by changing the mark emphasis. In collaboration with your students before each evaluation period, decide which criteria to retain and which to discard. You can even individualize the marking scheme for individual students to stimulate a specific aspect of growth. Students can help each other by reading designated sections of each other's response journals and discussing how well the criteria are being met and, perhaps, offering suggestions for improvement.

One of the most important features of response journals is that they supply concrete evidence of a process over time. To stimulate process objectives, you should include process as well as product criteria in your evaluation scheme.

Formative and summative evaluation

Perhaps this is the place to say a few words about formative and summative evaluation. (See **evaluation** in the glossary.) *Formative evaluation* is the ongoing assessment of student progress aimed almost exclusively at assisting students in their learning and at improving the educational experience. Such evaluation is geared to an individual's needs and personal growth. *Summative evaluation*, however, usually employs comparative standards and judgments in order to make an overall decision (e.g., any assessment made and recorded for report card purposes).

Most people assume that formative evaluation is a means to an end and that summative evaluation is an end in itself. If that were totally the case, summative evaluation would always be counter-productive to the learning process. In actual fact, if applied appropriately, summative evaluation can have an important formative outcome.

The key to turning summative evaluation into a powerful, positive force for learning lies in defining and declaring clear objectives - right up front for everyone to see, especially the students. If students know precisely the criteria by which they will be evaluated, they will more readily direct their efforts to meeting those criteria; if, in fact, students have the opportunity to set some of those criteria themselves, they can actually take over "ownership" for the learning.

Sample summative evaluation criteria

The following criteria for summative evaluation reflect the wide potential of response journals. The list, however is not meant to be exhaustive. The criteria you use will reflect your particular program objectives during a specific period.

To what extent do the entries indicate that the student has:

- kept a complete record of the titles of each independent reading selection and the amount read each period?

- included a variety of personal responses to reading selections?

- kept a complete record of media experiences (e.g., film, television, or video viewing) and responded to each in a thoughtful and reflective manner?

- kept a complete record of listening experiences (readalouds) and articulated personal reactions to each?

- kept track if his/her role in group discussions, reviewed past performances, and attempted to strengthen specific skills?

- recorded questions/comments/observations for later reference (e.g., for student/teacher conferences)?

- looked back at previous entries and attempted to reflect on those experiences/opinions/emotions?

Narrowing the focus

For a particular period, you may want to narrow the focus in order to stimulate a specific aspect of your program. In that case, you can adjust the criteria and the subsequent marks sheet.

The sample marks sheet on page 65 demonstrates how the evaluation criteria can be narrowed to emphasize and stimulate specific aspects of your program over a three- or four-week period.

Encouraging student input

If you want your students to "buy into" your program as quickly and as completely as possible, try including them in the process of devising evaluation criteria for marks! How much you do in this regard or when you start will depend on your individual class and your students' stage of readiness. You can ease into this process in a number of ways. For example,

- Brainstorm a list of criteria with your students. Through discussion, prioritize and short-list the items.

- To individualize the marking scheme, reserve a certain amount (perhaps 25%) for items not chosen by you. Ask each student to add items worth that amount to an individual marking scheme.

The sample marks sheet on page 66 shows how the teacher and student can each select criteria to be used in the teacher's evaluation for summative purposes.

The sample marks sheet on page 67 demonstrates how criteria from all functions of the response journal can be identified and used in a teacher's summative evaluation. Notice, as well, how criterion #5 is weighted to ensure attention.

Summative Evaluation Based on Selected Criteria

Independent Reading

Student's Name: _____

Evaluation Period: from _____ to _____

To what extent do your entries indicate that you have:

- kept a complete record of the titles of each independent
  reading selection and the amount read?   /25

- included a number of personal responses to independent
  reading selections (at least three per week)?   /25

- looked back at previous entries and attempted to reflect
  on those experiences/opinions/emotions?   /35

- recorded questions/comments/observations for student/
  teacher conferences?   /15
                                                           _____

                                          Total: ....../100

Comments:

_____

_____

_____

_____

_____

Summative Evaluation Based on Shared Criteria

Independent Reading

Student's Name: _____

Evaluation Period:from _____ to _____

Teacher-chosen criteria

To what extent do your entries indicate that you have:

- kept a complete record of the titles of each independent
  reading selection and the amount read? /20

- included a number of personal responses to independent
  reading selections (at least three per week)? /20

- looked back at previous entries and attempted to reflect
  on those experiences/opinions/emotions? /25

- recorded questions/comments/observations for student/
  teacher conferences? /10

Student-chosen criteria

To what extent do your entries indicate that you have:

- chosen and presented at least two readalouds to the class? /10

- read to younger students as part of a buddy-reading project? /10

- read a lot of different kinds of material for independent reading? /5

———

Total: ..../100

Comments:

_____

_____

_____

Summative Evaluation Based on Stated Criteria

Marking Response Journals

Student's Name: _____

Evaluation Period:　　from _____ to _____

1. Independent (Individual) Reading

	Complete				Incomplete	
• keeps daily records	5	4	3	2	1	0

	Beyond Requirements				Insufficient	
• reads sufficient amount	5	4	3	2	1	0

	Often				Never	
• varies responses	5	4	3	2	1	0

2. Readalouds/Media

	Always				Never	
• records and responds appropriately	5	4	3	2	1	0

3. Small-Group Discussions

	Always				Never	
• describes role objectively and thoroughly	5	4	3	2	1	0

	Often				Never	
• reviews past discussions and attempts to improve skills	5	4	3	2	1	0

4. Other Uses

	Often				Never	
• records questions/comments observations for other uses	5	4	3	2	1	0

5. In General

	Often				Never	
• looks back at, reflects on, and builds on previous entries	15	12	9	6	3	0

Comments:　　　　　　　　　　　　　　　　　　　　　　Mark: ..../50

_____

_____

_____

Formative self-evaluation

At regular intervals, ask your students to "step back" and evaluate their own responses on the basis of the outlined objectives. They can review their own progress, assess the extent to which they are meeting the objectives, and set new goals for themselves. At different times, you can have them isolate and examine one aspect of their journals or take an overall look at all aspects.

For students to assume an active role in the learning process, they need to see evaluation as a tool and to feel that they have control over its use. They need to understand how evaluation can help them and they need to practise self-evaluation on a regular basis. As they gain in confidence and skill, more mature students will often be able to apply their own criteria in their own way for their own purposes.

Most teachers, however, will need to consciously promote opportunities for their students to practise self-evaluation. The following sample forms demonstrate a few methods for initiating this kind of self-examination.

(See the sample formative self-evaluation charts on independent reading, small-group discussions, readalouds/media, and overall assessment on the following pages.)

Formative Self-Evaluation

Independent Reading

Student's Name: _____

Evaluation Period: from _____ to _____

1. How much have you read over this period? _____
   _____

2. What kind (s) of book (s) have you been reading? _____
   _____
   _____
   _____

3. How do you feel about the amount and type of reading you've been doing? (Please check one box and comment on why you feel that way.)

   Satisfied [_____]   Somewhat Satisfied [_____]   Dissatisfied [_____]

   _____
   _____
   _____

4. How do you feel about the kinds of responses you've been making to your reading? (Again, check one box and comment on why you feel that way.)

   Satisfied [_____]   Somewhat Satisfied [_____]   Dissatisfied [_____]

   _____
   _____
   _____

5. What goal(s) do you think you should set for your future reading?

   _____
   _____
   _____
   _____

Formative Self-Evaluation

Small-Group Discussions

Student's Name: _____

Evaluation Period: from _____ to _____

1. How many small-group discussions have you commented on during this period?
   _____

2. What kinds of things do you consistently do well during small-group discussions?
   _____
   _____
   _____
   _____

3. What kinds of things have you been improving on?
   _____
   _____
   _____
   _____

4. What is one skill you intend to work on in future discussions?
   _____
   _____
   _____
   _____

Formative Self-Evaluation

Readalouds/Media

Student's Name: _____

Evaluation Period: from _____ to _____

1. With which response are you most satisfied? Why?

_____

_____

_____

_____

2. With which response are you most dissatisfied? Why?

_____

_____

_____

_____

3. What can you try to do to make your responses generally more satisfying?

_____

_____

_____

_____

Formative Self-Evaluation

Overall Assessment

Student's Name: _____

Evaluation Period: from _____ to _____

How well do you think you've met the objectives for each of these components of your response journal?

	Completely				Insufficiently
1. Independent Reading	5	4	3	2	1
2. Readalouds/Media	5	4	3	2	1
3. Small-Group Discussions	5	4	3	2	1
4. Questions/Comments/Observations	5	4	3	2	1
5. Building on Previous Entries	5	4	3	2	1

For what area (s) should you set new goals?
_____
_____

How do you plan to meet the objectives in these areas more completely?
_____
_____
_____
_____
_____
_____

7 ∗ Response journals in the wider context

When journals first became popular in classrooms, they provided a forum both for individual, exploratory writing and for privileged, non-threatening dialogue, primarily with the teacher. In their journals, students could monitor and express their own "inner dialogues" as they reacted either to issues and events from the classroom curriculum and the wider world or to the significant experiences and emotions arising from their personal and private lives. This free-flowing "dialogue" could also be extended to teacher and peers as students felt a need to include others in their thoughts and deliberations. Sometimes they wrote to others for advice; sometimes they needed only a sympathetic and trusted reader.

Preserving vital functions

When students wrote to their teachers, the teachers often responded right in the students' journals. Other teachers thoughtfully used separate pieces of paper or "stick-on" message paper to let students decide whether or not to retain the reply in the journal. In any event, the journal acted as a safety valve for students, allowing them to tap powerful feelings and, when they were in the grip of serious and often confusing personal problems, to express those feelings to someone else. Although the implementation and maintenance of journals was often misguided, these functions of the journals were vitally needed. When using response journals, these same functions should be maintained.

Linking with people

In order to encourage this kind of personal writing and an exchange of perspectives, either student to student or student to teacher, a few basic guidelines need to be observed.

- *Response journals belong to the students.* This basic principle ensures the confidentiality of the private aspects of the response journals. Non-confidential content, such as what and how much a student reads, can certainly be shared with others at the teacher's discretion. Although the response journals are read and marked by the teacher, they are always returned to the student. Of course, if students choose to share the contents with others, they certainly may.

- Although "private" writing must never be marked either for content or form, the inclusion of such writing in the response journal could be valued with marks. If private writing is included in the criteria for evaluation, students will be more apt to view it as important. If that criterion is weighted appropriately, students will tend to engage in private writing only when they truly feel it's personally significant to do so.

- Students must be reassured that in spite of existing routines for reading response journals, teachers will always welcome and read a private entry at any time, if the student feels it's pressing and important enough to hand in. Such entries should be clearly marked *private*.

- With writing of a private nature, teachers must always respond in the role of trusted adult. In this role, teachers may often walk a tightrope with their comments. They need to advise but not command, disagree but not reject, and sympathize but not condone. In effect, they need to respond as adult friend to student friend.

Responding to Who You Are

Directions

Everyone needs a friend to talk to. But you don't have to have a friend in order to sort out what's on your mind. You can "talk about" your thoughts and feelings with yourself and with your teacher/reader - in your response journal. Remember to mark *private* in your response journal whenever you want to write in this fashion. Your private entries will never be shown to anyone else without your permission.

If you want your teacher (or a special friend in class) to read and reply to what you've written, simply hand it in (or hand it to your friend) and ask for a response. Unless you indicate otherwise, your teacher will reply on a separate, loose-leaf page or a"stick-on" message tab to allow you the option of keeping or not keeping the reply in your response journal.

When you decide to write this way, find a quiet spot and don't concern yourself with mechanics or neatness or even how well or how poorly you're wording your thoughts. Even a poorly-worded entry will get you in touch with your own thoughts and feelings and show you how you felt at a certain time, and that's the point of this kind of writing. Focus on the issue or feeling or idea and write whatever comes to mind. If you need a focus to begin, here are some suggestions.

• Explain your inner feelings. Try to put those feelings, good or bad, into words. This process can help you understand how your emotions work.

• Work out your problems. If you write about your worries, you may be able to understand more clearly what causes them.

• Explore ideas about life. Describe things you've noticed about human nature. Discuss your ideas of right and wrong. Tell what you think is important in life.

If you have something you want to write about but don't know how to start, try one of these phrases to get you going: Right now I feel…; Sometimes, I wonder if…; Some day, I'm going to…; I hate it when… .

Sample response to "Who You Are"

Private!!!   March 30

There's a lot of difference sometimes between how I act and
how I really feel. Like all this business you read and hear
about swarming in the malls. We talk about it sometimes and
my girlfriends say how awful it is but then they go ahead
and do what they've always done. I go along with them but I
don't feel too good about it. I think about what might happen
and I don't want to leave the house - ever! I've started
making up excuses not to go along with them. I think they
think something's weird with me. My dad says I should stay
home more and not go out until all this trouble blows over. It
would be great to feel safe all the time. Even going to school is
a hassle. I've got to take the bus and then walk. Guys are
always coming up to you and saying things. Who knows if
they have a knife or what's on their minds. Have you seen
knives in the school? I have. One of my friends says she saw
someone with a gun only she wouldn't recognize him again. I
don't want to lose my friends but I don't want to commit
suicide either. Do you get afraid? Do you still go to malls?
What do you think I should do?

                                                    - Debbie (age 15)

Linking with programs

Learning shouldn't be artificially compartmentalized. Even the organization of the school curriculum into separate subject areas has the potential for impeding learning. If the same teacher is responsible for presenting the program in all subject areas, organizational problems can be easily overcome. From the junior grades on, however, the various "disciplines" are increasingly assigned to different teacher-specialists. Bridging those disciplines and integrating programs then becomes vital to the promotion of effective and efficient learning. The word *integrated* is used so often in discussing English and language arts programs that the term needs clarification. The term is usually used in three ways.

- An *integrated* program is a blend of all the aspects of English: reading, writing, listening, speaking, viewing, valuing.

- An *integrated* program is an individualized program related to the personal growth, skills, and cultural needs of the individual student.

- An *integrated* program is co-ordinated with other aspects of a student's program, such as art, music or science. Conversely, the other aspects of a student's program should be integrated with the English program.

All three aspects of integration stem from the same concept about learning. In fact, "learning through language" is not just a "parenthood" statement. The process is detailed and specific and speaks as much to language programs as it does to learning "across the curriculum." As you reflect on the following basic principles of learning through language, consider how closely they match the principles involved in using response journals.

- To fully understand concepts, students need to "pick away" at ideas or "think aloud" in their own talk or style of writing. Opportunities to talk and write are crucial to real learning.

- Students should feel free to take risks in their writing. They need to write in their own words and feel confident that the meaning of what they say is the focal point of the writing experience.

- During the talking and writing process, ideas are being examined, analyzed, reformulated, and defined in very personal, individual, and essential ways.

- The jargon of specialized subjects and needlessly technical language tend to inhibit real learning.

- A variety of real audiences and a wide range of writing purposes will help students realize the need for writing.

The medium really is the message. With response journals, students can interact with issues and materials regardless of the subject area. The response journal forum is ideal for "examining, analyzing, reformulating, and defining" in a personal and individual manner. As the English or language arts teacher, you naturally welcome real problems to solve, opportunities for students to reflect on events, ideas, and values they're confronting every day, and the addition of real purposes for talking and writing. Whatever the subject area, the skills and goals are the same. If overlap occurs, it can only reinforce the learning. Since the English or language arts curriculum can itself become compartmentalized, we need to break down the barriers to real learning wherever they occur.

With this concept of integration in mind, try to capitalize on any opportunities to open the doors of your language classroom not only to the wider world beyond the school walls but also the often more isolated worlds of the subject-specialized curriculum. If you haven't already begun the process, you might want to try some of the following suggestions.

- Encourage students to comment in their journals on ideas and concepts from other subject areas. Perhaps they could write about questions that arise in history, a strong opinion they hold on a current issue, or impressions of a fictional character or historical figure who appeals to them.

- Suggest that students describe in their journals specific incidents and impressions arising from excursions, drama productions, or other special events. Then encourage them to re-read these specific entries and attempt to encapsulate their impressions, develop a more generalized viewpoint, or offer a revised perspective.

- Encourage students to use their response journals as a sounding board or trial run for writing for a variety of purposes and a wider audience.

- Encourage them to adapt their response journal entries for use in other areas of the writing program, for instance, as a starting-point for personal experience narrative or as the source for a letter.

- Provide opportunities for students who wish to share orally some of their response journal entries with a wider audience. These readings may stimulate lively discussion or result in a vital debate over issues raised.

From where does inspiration spring and what does student ownership of learning mean? The next response answers both questions as well as proving that the insights offered by personal response can happen anywhere and at any time.

Sample response to an observation

Thank you, Fred!   *March 7*

Let's be honest. I was totally bored. Writing was not my idea of a good time and I didn't know where to start. I checked my rough drafts and list of ideas and nothing turned me on. I just felt lazy and rusty and uninspired. I tried brainstorming. What can you get from a vacuum; I wanted to scream! No, this certainly wasn't my day until Fred came tripping up the aisle, flat on his face! It wasn't until he got up, tripped again, and sort of sprawled and stumbled into his seat that the idea came. The way Fred had dramatically fallen reminded me of the time I went skiing and the hilarious time my friends and I had. You wouldn't believe the fall I took and what happened after that! Sometimes I wish I kept a diary. Anyway, thank you, Fred!

- Shana P. (age 13)

In this entry, notice the value of peer-response partners as well as the sense of ownership as the writer makes an important discovery about authors and the "originality" of their material.

Sample response to a writing period

Writing Log　　　　　　　　　　　　　　*November 26*

I did something today with a story that I've never done before. Ralph was reading over the latest version of my story "Dark Spaces". He liked the way things were going until he mentioned that the story sort of jumps in the middle of the action and he couldn't follow what was going on. I looked it over and realized he was dead on. That's when the idea flashed into my head. I didn't even want Ralph to continue reading. You see, over the summer I had started a story similar to this one but it was called something else and I hadn't thought about it for a while. By combining the two, I solved the problem Ralph had found and also made the story more descriptive and more exciting. Stealing from yourself is great! Now all I have to do is steal a better ending somewhere. Ralph says he saw the ending coming from about the second paragraph. Maybe it's time to switch readers!

- Bill L. (age 12)

8 * Checklists for planning the classroom environment

To be fully effective, response journals need to become an integral part of a flexible, integrated classroom environment. The recursive nature of reading/writing processes do not permit easy "pigeon-holing". Processing language is also unpredictable. As much as you try to plan and organize the process, language tends to spill over the edges of your timetable and "wrinkle" your routines. When that happens, you need to emphasize the function and let the form adapt.

The function of any classroom activity is simply stated - meaning. The focal point is the meaning a student is deriving from print and talk, the meaning encapsulated in his/her writing, and the meaning of what she/he says. The idea of personal response depends on individualization and supports the concepts of self-direction and personal growth.

An effective language program needs an atmosphere conducive to language activity. To learn about language, students need to use language; they need to talk and listen and read and write as much as possible. The classroom must become a place for processing language. Teaching the mechanics of language is an important component of the process as long as it happens in the context of a student's actual language and as long as it never obscures or devalues the primary focus on meaning.

Regardless of the shape your program takes, it must accommodate a wide range of individual reading levels. Your students have a right to reading materials that suit their individual abilities. Your program must also accommodate a wide range of individual interests. Students need daily opportunities to read, talk, listen to, and write about themes with which they can personally relate. Each student is leading a specific and particular life; if you can make contact with that life and tap it, the language will flow.

The main components

If you can answer "yes" to each of the following questions, your program is well-balanced, vital, and student-centred. The checklist might also give you an idea or two for fine-tuning your program.

Does your program:

- include large blocks of time for language arts or English?

- include daily opportunities for readalouds, independent, self-selected reading, personal response, writing as process, reading/writing conferences?

- ensure that learning often occurs co-operatively in pairs, small groups, combined groups, and, when appropriate, as a whole-class group?

- ensure that drama is employed whenever possible to facilitate learning?

- encourage a warm, supportive, accepting atmosphere, free of sexist, racist, cultural, and ability stereotypes?

- encourage students to make decisions and choices and accept a developing degree of responsibility for what, when, how, and where they learn?

- include the teacher actively reading/writing and, then, sharing with the students how he/she actually goes about the process?

- operate with flexible seating/work areas to facilitate co-operative learning?

- include additional school and community human resources, e.g., teacher-librarian (resource-based learning), authors, storytellers?

Essential materials

Personal response may be severely limited by the availability of materials and equipment. The broader the range and variety of stimulating experiences, the greater the chance that the incredible spectrum of individual differences in any one classroom can be accommodated. You can review the choices your students have with the following checklist.

Your students should have access to many different types of print materials at different levels of difficulty and with a variety of themes. How many of these does your classroom have?

- novels (many individual titles)
- newspapers
- poetry
- picture books
- dictionaries
- anthologies
- magazines
- informational books
- student-written material
- thesauri

Are all of the following categories represented?

- legends
- fairy tales
- myths
- folk tales
- plays
- a variety of genre, e.g., mystery, adventure, science fiction, exposition
- books and articles related to the "content" areas, e.g., history, science

How available are audio-visual equipment and resources?

- audio tapes for listening and recording
- video tapes for viewing and recording
- films, filmstrips, overhead projector
- film and video catalogues
- television listings
- a television set
- computer for word processing; printer

Glossary

The definitions in this selected glossary reflect the meanings that are used in the text.

brainstorming: generating a list of examples, ideas, or questions to illustrate, expand, or explore a central idea or topic (record all ideas; no evaluating of ideas during collecting; quantity of ideas is important; encourage students to expand on each other's ideas; "zany" ideas are welcome).

conferencing: opportunities to discuss ideas and problems in pairs or small groups; conferences can be conducted in a variety of formats with and without the teacher.

contact: agreement a student makes to complete an assigned/under-taken unit of work within a given period of time; usually signed by student and teacher.

co-operative learning: a variety of small-group instructional techniques focussing on peer collaboration.

co-operative planning: planning by the classroom teacher and the teacher-librarian of a unit of study in which aims, objectives, teaching strategies, and research and study skills are included. The unit is taught and evaluated by both classroom teacher and teacher-librarian.

"cueing" response: a guiding suggestion or hint that gives an individual a sense of the kinds of responses possible. The "cues" serve as examples or models. Individuals are encouraged to develop their own responses based on their own purposes for reading and their personal perspectives as independent readers.

diagnostic evaluation: an aspect of formative evaluation; becoming familiar with each student's interests, abilities, preferred learning style, and learning difficulties.

diary (private): an in-class record of personal observations, random jottings, and a daily record of thoughts and feelings; shared only if the student agrees; difficult to maintain over time or adapt for use in other parts of the writing program (see also **journal, log**).

evaluation: determining progress toward and attainment of specific goals; assessing student progress and achievement and program effectiveness (see also **diagnostic evaluation, formative evaluation,** and **summative evaluation**).

expressive mode: includes such forms as sharing personal experiences, personal response writing, exploratory writing, projecting into the experience of another, personal letters.

formative evaluation: the ongoing assessment of student progress aimed almost exclusively at assisting learning and at improving the educational experience; geared to an individual's needs and personal growth.

holistic mark: a general-impression mark given after one reading.

integrated program: a term used in three different ways: an integrated program can refer to a blend of all the aspects of English: reading, writing, listening, speaking, viewing, valuing; also, an individualized program related to the personal growth, skills, and cultural needs of the individual student; as well, a program co-ordinated with other aspects of a student's program: art, music, science, etc.

journal (public): a less private form of diary; is more readily shared, allows more flexibility, and is more adaptable as a teaching tool; especially useful when used to elicit personal responses to reading and issues and events under study and when the writing is used in other parts of the writing program (see also **diary, log**).

literacy: basically the ability to read and write; extended today to include the processing of information from all sources and systems, including electronic and microelectronic.

literature: writing of high quality and significance because of a successful integration of components such as style, organization, language, and theme.

log: a calendar-like record of the events of a day or a week (see also **journal, diary**).

"making meaning": the recognition that the act of processing language involves more than the communicating or recording of experience; through language we tend to construct our sense of things by clarifying, discovering, assessing, reflecting on, resolving, and refining what we really think and feel about experience.

personal reading: reading self-selected materials; also, reading material which may be suggested by someone else but which is so interesting and stimulating that the student becomes independently engaged by the experience.

personal response: encouraging students to begin an explication of and reflection on material with their own idiosyncratic, immediate, and spontaneous impressions, reactions, and questions where and when they arise; includes the recognition that our listening, speaking, reading, writing, viewing and thinking processes are directed toward "making meaning" (see "**making meaning**", above).

personal writing: writing about self-selected issues and events arising from an individual's daily life or interests; also, any writing that involves a student to such an extent that he/she is independently motivated to complete the experience.

poetic mode: includes stories, poems, patterning from literature.

readalouds: any material read aloud, usually by the teacher; students of all ages should be read to regularly; readalouds should0 comprise both fiction and non-fiction and should be drawn from a variety of genres.

reading as process: the recognition that reading is an active, personal, and recursive process integral to an individual's ongoing investigation into experience and that the process requires the integration of listening, speaking, writing, viewing, and thinking with reading to be fully effective.

response journal: a notebook or folder in which students record their personal reactions to, questions about, and reflections on what they read, view, listen to, and discuss in addition to how they actually go about reading, viewing, listening, and discussing.

risk-taking: the internalized understanding that mistakes/approximations are *good;* the freedom to experiment, extend the known, or try something new without unduly worrying about failing or being wrong.

summative evaluation: usually employs comparative standards and judgments in order to make an overall decision (e.g., any assessment made and recorded for report card purposes).

transactional mode: focuses on providing information; includes reports, instructions, arguments, scientific observations, business letters.

whole language: a learning/teaching approach that emphasizes the integration of language "threads" (i.e., listening, speaking, reading, writing, thinking) within the context of meaningful communication (e.g., a single writing task may engage a student in a range of discussion, composing, editing/revising, reading tasks); includes the idea of moving away from isolated, fragmented approaches such as a regular "grammar" period outside the context of the writing process.

writing as process: the recursive and blended elements of writing: pre-writing, writing, post-writing; includes writing for actual audiences other than the teacher and for purposes other than summative evaluation.

writing folder: a folder or notebook organized to accommodate and facilitate the various stages in the writing process; sometimes used as a synonym for writing as process (see **writing as process**).

writing modes: identified as expressive, poetic, and transactional; all modes can be accommodated within the response journal format (see also **expressive mode, poetic mode**, and **transactional mode**).

A selected and annotated bibliography

The following titles represent only a few of the many, fine teacher references available to guide and support classroom programs and are not meant to be exhaustive or even representative in any way. In the best tradition of personal response and for a variety of reasons, aspects of these specific references helped the author better understand the power and potential of personal response.

Atwell, Nancie. *In the Middle: Writing, Reading, and Learning with Adolescents*. Portsmouth, New Hampshire: Boynton/Cook Publishers, 1987. (One teacher's personal narrative of how she worked her way through to a better understanding of how to help her students "make meaning"; presents a real teacher with real students in a real classroom.)

Dias, Patrick. *Making Sense of Poetry: Patterns in the Process*. Ottawa, Ontario: CCTE (Canadian Council of Teachers of English), 1987. (Presents a compelling technique for allowing students to "unlock" poetry in their own way through peer-discussion groups.)

Metropolitan Toronto School Board. *Together We Learn*. Willowdale, Ontario, 1988. (A comprehensive, step-by-step handbook explaining how to use small-group, co-operative learning strategies.)

Miles, Matthew. *Learning to Work in Groups: A Practical Guide for Members and Trainers. 2nd ed.* New York: Teacher's College Press, 1981. (Although this "training" guide is not intended for application in classrooms or with students, chapters 1, 2, and 7 contain clearly outlined, group-learning concepts and practical, skills-oriented approaches invaluable to classroom teachers.)

Spear, Karen. *Sharing Writing: Peer Response Groups in English Classes*. Portsmouth, New Hampshire: Boynton/Cook Publishers, 1988. (Highlights the use of peer response in writing classes. The principles apply directly to co-operative discussion groups.)

Thomson, Jack. *Understanding Teenagers' Reading: Reading Processes and the Teaching of Literature*. New York: Nichols Publishing

Co., 1987. (Places personal response in an historical context and establishes the theoretical and research foundation for personal response approaches.)